Joshua's Ring

Joshua's Ring

As told by
Rosemary and Joseph Wilker
to
Marie Murphy Duess

Joshua's Ring

For more information, visit
www.MarieDuess.com/Joshua_s_Ring.html
or
www.joshuasring.com

Printing History: First Printing 2013

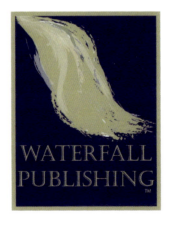

PRINTED IN THE UNITED STATES OF AMERICA
10 9 8 7 6 5 4 3 2 1

for
Austin and Erin

"And they can no longer die;

for they are like the angels.

They are God's children,

since they are children of the resurrection."

Luke 20:36

Joshua Joseph Wilker
September 12, 1988 - March 4, 2003

Introduction

He didn't want to die. He didn't want to be known for miracles. He didn't want to do anything more remarkable than any other boy would. He just wanted to live an ordinary life, with the normal dreams of every boy—the typical desires, concerns, and hopes of every boy.

His parents didn't want him to die. The only miracle they looked for was one that would save his life and make him well so that he could live and grow to manhood.

This is a story that is told too often by too many parents of children who are diagnosed with life-threatening disease and lose their battle against death. Yet this story, perhaps like others, has a rather remarkable outcome...not an ending, but a continuation. In the end it is a testament that these children didn't lose to death, but triumphed over it.

I knew Joshua Wilker, but I didn't know him well. I remember him mostly as an adorable preschooler with curly, golden-brown hair, big expressive eyes, and a personality that made you smile just looking at him. I remember him performing with his Kindergarten classmates at the annual Christmas show at Grey Nun Academy, where my own children, both of whom were older than Josh, went to school. I remember Joshua's class singing Jingle Bells, and Josh a little more enthusiastic about "jingling" than the rest, and eventually crossing his legs until the song finished. I recall his father, the gym teacher and athletic coach at the school, grimacing and running his hand over his face as the audience convulsed in laughter while his little guy ran quickly to the boys' room immediately after the performance.

Seven years later, I remember hearing that this sweet, funny, charming little boy was being treated for leukemia. I remember choking back tears, my heart breaking for his father, Joe, who I knew well from my own affiliation with the school, and for his mother, Rosemary, who I worked with on numerous fundraising committees at Grey Nun Academy.

There are always "signs" when someone dies. It's very common to hear of synchronicities that happen after the passing of a human being. It's happened to me with several of my own loved ones. I will admit that I wanted to see these signs. I looked for them; I longed for them because they were a comfort for me. So as much as I "believe" in them, I have always wondered if these "signs" are perhaps just a human being's way of surviving heartbreak.

When Josh died in March of 2003, I decided my family would purchase a special gift rather than send flowers to commemorate his life. My husband and I discussed buying altar vestments that could be used by the chaplain or visiting priests in the chapel of Grey Nun Academy in remembrance of Josh. He was in the eighth grade at the private Catholic elementary school when he died, and we knew that this gift would bring Josh to mind for everyone who knew and loved him when worn at special liturgies like First Eucharist Celebrations and Graduations.

The night before I went to the religious article store, I had a dream that I was in the chapel at Grey Nun Academy, but all I could see was the altar. On the altar were a chalice and paten and what I believed to be priest's hands cupped around them but not touching them. There was a defect on the chalice—a little scratch. I mentioned the dream to my husband when I awakened the next morning. "You must have dreamed that because we were talking about the vestments," my husband said.

I went to the store to pick out the vestments, and as I passed a case that housed brand new chalices and other altar vessels, I saw the chalice that was in my dream—defect and all. I was stunned...absolutely blown away. A sign? For me? I barely knew the boy. I certainly wasn't looking for a sign from Joshua—not that I didn't care about him and his parents, but because I just wouldn't expect a sign from him since I was a stranger to him.

Needless to say, I purchased the damaged chalice, as well as the paten that sat beside it on the shelf and ignored the numerous other perfect vessels. What would his parents think about me giving them something less than perfect to commemorate their son's life? How could I do that? I could do it because I knew without any doubt that Josh had picked it out. I did purchase the vestments and included a note to Joe and Rosemary trying to explain why I would have the audacity to give them a chalice and paten that were slightly damaged.

"They're going to think I'm crazy," I told my husband.

"Maybe," he replied, "or they're going to think we're too cheap to buy a perfect chalice."

"I'm giving it to them anyway," I told him, "because it wasn't my decision, it was Josh's."

His parents were very gracious and, in fact, expressed that they had had some very exceptional "signs" of their own.

Although I thought of Joe and Rosemary and their other children from time to time after Josh's funeral and prayed for them whenever I did, I didn't have any correspondence with them after Josh's death. My children, Mai-Ann and Buddy, had already graduated from the elementary school before Josh died, and we were not socially linked with the Wilkers. The school was our only connection.

Then, in early 2006, there was a phone message on our answering machine from Rosemary asking me to return her call. There was something she wanted to discuss. I didn't return her call right away. I listened to the message, wondered about it, then moved on to my next chore, my next project, and the next day. A few days later I was straightening up my home office, moved some books from one side of a shelf to the other, and a piece of paper fluttered down onto my foot.

It was the prayer card from Josh's funeral. I called Rosemary right then.

"I want you to help me write about Josh and some things that have happened since he died," she told me.

The prayer card was still in my hand and I looked down at it.

No. The word formed in my mind before she finished her sentence, and was followed by a rush of more negative thoughts. *No, I don't write that well. I'm not talented enough. I'm too busy working in a very demanding job. No, I just won't do it right. I just lost my sister-in-law...I have to help care for her two young boys. No, no, no... I don't think this is a good idea right now. I don't want to write this sad, sad story.*

I never said these things to Rosemary.

I turned the prayer card over: *In Loving Memory of Joshua J. Wilker, September 12, 1988 – March 4, 2003 ... What kind of place would Heaven be with all its streets of gold, if all the souls that dwell up there like yours and mine were old?*

"Sure, Rosemary, of course I will," I told her.

Suddenly, my apprehension did not matter because I believe that Joshua Joseph Wilker wanted me to tell his story from his parents' perspective—from his parents' hearts. And that's what I'm doing.

Josh Wilker didn't want to die. He didn't want to be known for signs or miracles. I didn't want to ever have to write a story about a boy who died too young or the miraculous events that have occurred since his death.

Sometimes we are led on journeys to places that we had not imagined we would take.

Chapter One

What kind of place would Heaven be
With all its streets of gold,
If all the soul's that dwell up there,
Like yours and mine were old?
How strange would heaven's music sound
When harps begin to ring,
If children were not gathered round
To help the angels sing.
The children that God sends to us
Are only just on loan.
He knows we need their sunshine
To make a house a home.
We need the inspiration of
a baby's blessed smile,
He doesn't say they've come to stay,
Just lends them for a while.
Sometimes it takes them years to do
The work for which they come.
Sometimes in just a month or two
Our Father calls them home.
I like to think the souls up there
Bear not one sinful scar.
I love to think of heaven as
A place where children are.

From the back of the prayer card given out at Joshua's funeral.

Author not credited.

Chapter Two

From Josh's 8th Grade Language Arts Journal

September, 2002

My Goals

1. Get into LaSalle or Holy Ghost Prep High School.

2. Get a scholarship to any one of these high schools.

3. Become class president.

4. Get straight A's or have an A/B average.

5. Get along with other people as they do [to] me.

6. Hand in all my homework.

January 22, 2003

(Last entry in journal)

3 Wishes

1.   To be rich

2.   To have super powers

3.   To [be cures] for all sickness

Joshua's Ring

The Autobiography of Joshua Wilker (exactly as he wrote it)

As I entered this world, I remember bright lights. This light was the beginning of a great life for me. The day was Monday, September 12, 1988. This was the second day of my father's new career as a Health and Physical Education teacher at a private school. Who would of knew that this job would be a very significant part of my own life today? He had graduated in 1986 with a teaching degree, but at that time teaching jobs were hard to come by. This was an exciting time for both him and my mother. A new job in a position he had worked hard to get and a new baby on the way.

The events that happened that day were exciting and of course with my family unusual. My mother was expecting to have me on September 5th, but here it was a bright and sunny Monday morning and finally the time had arrived. She called my father out of school at about 1:00 p.m. Everyone was excited. By 4:00 p.m. my grandmother was there; nothing yet. The doctor decides by about 7:00 p.m. they were going to deliver me by C-section. My dad made the doctor promise that he would deliver me and have my mom back in her room in time for Monday night football. This was also a big event. The Eagles would be playing the Phoenix Cardinals for the first Monday night game of the season.

As promised, I was born at 8:05 p.m. and my mom was in her room watching the Eagles bring home a victory. It was an all-around tremendous day for a lot of people, but mostly a day that my parents will always cherish. My name is Joshua Joseph Wilker and this is my story.

As you can imagine, my father and mother are avid sports fans. I have definitely inherited their love of sports. From the time I could walk I have always been involved in physical activities and sports. My parents spend a lot of time with me in the yard and going to parks. The first house we lived in had a built-in pool. So they were teaching me to swim before I could even walk. I am sure one of my first words was ball. For my first Christmas I had a sports net that looked like a soccer net with a basketball net on one side and a baseball hanging from the other side.

The year I turned two, my parents moved to the house we currently live in today. It is a great neighborhood and I have a lot of friends. My best friend lives across the street from me. His name is also Josh and we have been friends since my family moved here. Together we have a lot of other friends in the neighborhood. I usually enjoy going to their houses and playing sports, video games or just hanging out watching TV or listening to music. Sometimes we get together and make videos outside. My all time favorite thing to do that we do almost every night, especially in the summertime, is play manhunt.

I have a younger brother and sister. Their names are Austin and Erin. They are really cool. There is five years between me and Austin and eight years between me and Erin. Believe it or not they play manhunt with us along with their friends. My parents definitely picked a great place for us to grow up.

At the age of three my father surprised us with a boxer puppy. We named him Zonka. This was after a famous football player named Larry Zonka who played for the Miami

Joshua's Ring

Dolphins. We only had him for about a year. I loved that dog and still remember him vividly. He was like Houdini, though, he could get out of our yard no mater what we did to the fence. I can remember my mother chasing him through the neighborhood with cheese trying to catch him and bring him home. Unfortunately, my mother did not love him as much as my dad and I because one weekend when my dad was at Notre Dame seeing a Fighting Irish football game, my mother gave him to an all-breed rescue. So he is now somewhere in Rochester, New York. Also in my lifetime we had two guinea pigs named Pinky and The Brain. This was another chore for my mother but lucky for her they died naturally after about a year. Presently I have fish. This is a job for my father, so I hope to have them around much longer.

Let's see, when I turned four, my father officially enrolled me in soccer and I continue playing on the school team and a travel team to this day. I love this sport. I pretty much play this year round. It officially starts in the fall and continues into the spring, then during the winter I play on an indoor team. I think I love playing indoor soccer the best. Soccer is an exciting sport but indoor there is not as much of the ball going out of bounds since you can play the ball off the wall.

I started playing baseball when I was five and when I was nine I was named the best and most improved player on my team. Baseball was not my favorite sport. So by the time I was ten I just did not want to play on a baseball team anymore.

My all time favorite sport is basketball. I currently play on the school team and for Upper Makefield travel. I pretty much play everyday and we have a small court out in the backyard. I also love football but only play for fun. My life is sort of normal, I guess. I am now 13 and as you probably could guess, my Dad is still teaching at the same school (Grey Nun Academy) and this is where I am today. My friends here are really cool too. Most of them I have been friends with since pre-school. We like to go to the movies together, play football and basketball, and go to parties. We all get along well for the most part.

My family has gone on many vacations, but of course my favorite one was going to Disney World. For the most part we spend a lot of the time in the summer at the shore. We are fortunate enough to have good friends that have a house on the beach. These good friends have been my father's friends since he was in elementary school and they are like family to us. We consider them relatives and I am good friends with their sons who are my age and, of course, love sports. I foresee being this close with them when I am my father's age.

I am writing this after a long holiday weekend at the shore. I would love to be a professional athlete one day. I can't predict my future but I can work to build a solid one. This is my life and how I've lived it out to this day. So I hope you've enjoyed this little segment on me and had fun reading about me. Oh yeah, always remember to live life out to the fullest.

By Joshua Wilker

Joshua's Ring

Chapter Three

Joshua was born on September 12, 1988. Robust would be a good word for him. A sturdy built round boy with red cheeks and his father's curly hair. He was a good kid, a sweet gentle boy, who was very likable.

People have the tendency to remember those who have died as "saints," whether they were or not, and the best attributes would be applied to children most especially. Yet we all know that kids aren't always saints. In fact, children can be the cruelest of human beings, especially to each other, for inexplicable reasons. Joshua was a normal child, who argued with his younger siblings, Austin and Erin, just like all boys do, and he had small disputes with his friends and classmates. He felt anger, frustration, annoyance; he was a normal person.

But the truth is Joshua was nicer than most—more patient, kinder. He had a great laugh and a good outlook on life. He loved to have fun, he loved to play basketball and soccer, he loved to watch the Sixers' games and the Eagles, he loved going to the Jersey shore, and he liked school (except for the hard tests). He also loved to run in the rain with complete abandon.

Josh was religious, devoutly so for someone so young. That isn't necessarily unusual since he was born and reared by good Catholics who have a solid faith, but Josh's faith in God and his devotion to the Mother of God was exceptional for his age and gender, even before he became ill. In fact, if he heard of someone who was ill, he'd say a rosary for them—not common for a junior high school-aged kid.

As mentioned before, Josh was enrolled in Grey Nun Academy in Yardley, Pennsylvania—the same school where his father taught—when he was four years old, and since it is a small private Catholic school, the classes are kept to no more than 25 children in a class. Usually, one or two may leave before 8th grade, and some new children will take their place, but most of the time the students are together for the full ten years. They are more like siblings than classmates, which usually results in sibling-like quarrelling. Yet, Josh was able to keep out of the quarrelling because of his good nature and the fact that he was just so likable.

During his childhood, Josh was unusually healthy and suffered only minor colds and occasional sore throats. He had perfect attendance at school.

In November of 2002, Joshua was kicked in the knee while playing sports. His father's best friend, who is also the family's physician, Dr. J.T. Kane, treated the knee and told Josh to take it easy and stay off it for a few days. Josh followed his "uncle's" orders, but he continued to limp. Two weeks later his mother noticed that it was Josh's other knee

5

that was swollen and bothering him. Still, Joshua insisted upon playing basketball for his school team on November 4, 2002, and received Player of the Game that night. His basketball jersey number was 11.

The next day he felt lightheaded. Dr. Kane took blood. The results were alarming. His white cells were greatly elevated, and Dr. Kane asked an oncologist, Dr. Jane Minturn, at Children's Hospital of Pennsylvania (CHOP) to see Josh immediately. In fact, before J.T. even spoke with Rosemary and Joe, he had made the arrangements for Josh to go to CHOP that very day. When Josh arrived at CHOP, he was already scheduled for a spinal tap and X-rays.

The diagnosis was Acute Lymphoblastic Leukemia (ALL), which is a cancer of the white blood cells—the myeloid cells. The very next day he started treatment as an inpatient. He stayed in the hospital throughout the month of November receiving chemotherapy for four weeks. Then he would go back every Tuesday for chemotherapy until January 28, 2003.

After that date, Josh was going to be given a short three-week break before he had to begin his next course of treatment. But there would be no "breather" for Josh or his parents.

Please understand that this story is not about Josh's suffering. It is about messages that he has given to those who love him, and even to those who didn't know him, to let them know that he has triumphed over suffering. Yet, the story would not be complete if we didn't know what he went through during the last month of his life. We wouldn't have the knowledge to understand why this story is important, and so we must touch upon what happened to this precious human being and comprehend his strength, his parents' strength, his belief in God, in the Holy Rosary, and in his ring.

After Josh's diagnosis and all through his treatment, Josh prayed the rosary. He was given the rosary by his aunt, and he had it with him all the time. Additionally, a neighbor who Josh had prayed the rosary for when she was ill and who knew how devoted Josh was to the Blessed Mother, gave him a ring that was fashioned after a decade of the rosary with a crucifix that sits on top of the finger. Joshua loved it, and he never took it off again except when he had to. The beautiful faith he exhibited—even though he was a young teenager in an age when most kids scoff at overt acts of religion—inspired others, including his own family and teachers.

Throughout Joshua's illness, from diagnosis through chemotherapy and radiation, his faith was unfaltering. He never asked *why me?* He never suggested that God was doing this to him. He just prayed. He simply believed and lived the words, "Thy will be done."

On Wednesday, January 29, Josh told his mother his body hurt. Rosemary called Dr. Minturn and she assured Rosemary that because his immune system was so low at that point she wouldn't be surprised if he might have picked up a virus. The doctor advised Rosemary to give him lots of fluid and if he ran a fever or started to have nosebleeds to bring him into the Emergency Room at CHOP.

On Thursday, January 30, his body hurt more, but there was no fever, no nosebleed, and Josh was not having any trouble drinking, so the doctor still advised to keep him home and watch him closely.

On Friday, his body hurt so much that he didn't want to be touched. Rosemary called the doctor again, but there were no symptoms of infection and because his immune system was so compromised, it was decided that it was probably best not to bring him to the hospital where he would not be as comfortable as he was at home.

Rosemary recalls, "I was trying to comfort him. He was lying in his bed and I asked him if there was anything I could do for him. 'Can you heal me?' he asked, and I apologized and told him that only God could heal him. All I could do was try to make him comfortable. He just said thanks and rolled over. I will never forget that moment. I almost think at that point he decided he wanted to be with God."

Rosemary also wrote in her journal, "Josh has daydreamed about God and Heaven ever since he was a little boy. About a month before he was diagnosed with ALL, he was on his bed and I thought he was studying. I asked him if he wanted me to study with him and he replied that he was just lying there daydreaming. I asked what he was daydreaming about and he said, 'What it would be like to be in heaven.' Then he threw his arms out like wings and said, 'You're free; you can do whatever you want.'"

On both Thursday and Friday nights, Rosemary slept in Josh's room to be near him if he needed her. In the middle of the night on Friday, he started to hallucinate. He awakened a couple of times laughing and talking to himself. At one point he thought his little brother Austin was in the room. Yet, he wasn't raving or distressed. In fact his mother remembers that Josh was in really good spirits throughout that night even in his delirium.

On Saturday morning he was running a fever, and his parents took him to CHOP immediately. He was so weak he couldn't walk. The ER staff put Josh into isolation to avoid his catching anything, and the hospital staff determined that he was dehydrated and started IV fluids immediately.

Josh and his parents were in the ER most of the day and he started to feel better. By afternoon, he was able to walk around and use the bathroom himself. Joe and Rose were overwhelmed with relief seeing him so much better.

It's strange the things that we remember after experiencing a traumatic experience. When everything else should be blotted out of our minds, there will be some one thing outside the realm of our personal anguish that we focus on and recall. For the Wilkers, the day that starts what they refer to as the "lost days," they also remember was the day the space shuttle Columbia exploded over Texas on its re-entry into the Earth's atmosphere. It was Saturday, February 1, 2003, and all of the members of the crew were killed.

At around 8:30 that night Rosemary left the hospital and went to her parents to pick up their younger children, Austin and Erin, while Joe stayed with his son.

This was not the first time Joe had experienced the terror of cancer and the fear of losing a loved one. Both of his parents had died when Joe was young—his father when

Joe was a child and his mother when he was just 21. He had taken a leave of absence from college to care for his mother when she was in the end stage of cancer. The ugly claws of the disease and the hovering shadow of death were no strangers to Joe; still, he was optimistic throughout Josh's diagnosis and treatment. This time would be different. This time it was his son and only a different outcome from that of his parents would be acceptable to this down-to-earth, rough-and-ready sports coach. He would "will" his son healthy again if it were possible.

At 10:30 that night, the hospital called Rosemary. A nurse in the Intensive Care Unit called to inform her that they had moved Josh to her unit instead of to the oncology ward. The nurse explained that he had received too much fluid in the ER, and it had overflowed into his lungs. They needed to try to dry out his lungs with oxygen. Rosemary swallowed down her anger and fear and answered the questions concerning Josh's medical history to fill in any gaps Joe may have forgotten. In the morning when she called, Joe told her not to bring their younger children to the hospital to see Josh as she had planned. Josh had had a bad night and was pulling at the oxygen mask and thrashing around. Joe informed Rosemary that he had been told that the hospital personnel were thinking of putting Josh on a respirator for one day to dry his lungs faster.

When Rosemary arrived at the hospital at around 9 a.m. on Monday morning, she found several physicians near the door of Josh's room. They appeared to be arguing. She was to find out later that the oncologists were upset because Josh had not been isolated in ICU and he now had a respiratory syncytial virus (RSV), which he didn't have when he had entered the hospital the day before. RSV infects the lungs and breathing passages, and although it's fairly common in young children, it can be seriously dangerous to anyone with a weakened immune system.

This was to be the beginning of a chain of events that prevented Josh from being discharged from the hospital—indeed, to regain his strength at all.

Chapter Four

Joe decided to keep a journal for Josh. He wanted his son to know all about the days he spent in the hospital from that first week so that Josh would understand all that he had been through and how he had fought back with as much strength as was humanly possible.

Joe and Rosemary took photographs of Josh during that time. When he was well again, they would let him read the journal and would show him the photographs. They felt it would be something he'd want to know; something he deserved to read and see once he was well again.

Joe titled this journal, Lost Days, and it begins,

"Dear Josh,
This is a journal that I am keeping while you are in the hospital."

Almost every day while Josh was at CHOP during this time, Joe kept track of what transpired.

Saturday, 2/1/03: You ate your breakfast and went back to sleep—you seemed a little bit better but were really tired…that is expected as a result of your radiation treatment which ended Christmas Eve. We took your temperature at 1:00 p.m., it was 102, so we called down to CHOP and they said to bring you in…

Sunday, 2/2/03: They tried to give you air through tubes in your nose, but they felt you were not getting enough oxygen so they tried a mask called a C-Pap, but you were fighting it…they said you were fighting the machine so much and making your lungs work harder so they decided to put a tube in your mouth to make it easier for you to breath and take the pressure off how hard you were working. But you had fluid in your lungs which was not allowing you to use your lungs to full capacity, so the ventilator helped to keep your lungs extended and dry them out…To get off the ventilator they want all your readings to be at five…at this time they put petrolatum opth ointment in your eyes because you were not able to close them when you were sedated…you were heavily sedated and given blood transfusions and two bags of platelets…intermittently the air tube was suctioned which you didn't like at all because it makes you gag…they placed an IV in both of your arms and an arterial line in your groin area and this is where they take blood that leaves your heart.

Each day, Joe records Josh's condition, the meds he was given, the stream of physicians and medical specialists who visited the room.

Dobutamine...Dopamine...Lorazepam... you sleep 12 to 15 hours a day... your ANC was near 0 and your platelets were real low and you are susceptible to catching something...now you have E-Coli virus in your blood stream... Vancomycin... Gentamicin... Fentanyl...still sedated and intubated, and your stomach was distended and they think there's a possible abscess...added Flagyl because you now have a fungus from the tube in your mouth...

The journal entries are heartbreaking and difficult to read. Joshua remained on the ventilator and was taken for numerous tests including C.A.T. scans, echocardiograms, and ultra sounds to look for blood clots. And mixed in with all of these accounts of medical procedures and updates on Josh's condition, which was dire, Joe includes news from the world outside Josh's hospital room, an indication that through all of it, Joe always believed Josh would be fine and would want to know what he missed while so grievously ill.

It snowed this afternoon, just a little, but you know Grey Nun Academy, it let out early...there was a two hour delay at school today because of black ice.... you have a lot of emails from your class...yesterday the nation was put on a state of alert because we are building up our forces to attack Iraq and our allies France and Germany said we should give the inspectors more time to find chemical weapons but Bush is getting pissed off...it snowed a little last night, but they are expecting a lot more Sunday...

And from time to time there was good news from the physicians.

Well, last night was good. You were sleeping great...and your lungs were clear...you have been breathing very well since they cleaned out your tubes...the surgeon was here about 6:00 a.m. and confirmed that the CAT showed that you have inflammation of the intestines...both oncology and surgery agreed that you did not have an abscess and no surgery is needed...just treating it with antibiotics...your belly went down which is a great sign...

The roller coaster ride continued. Josh had good nights; he had bad nights. Joe recorded that Josh was greatly agitated much of the time and did a lot of thrashing in his bed. The physicians added new meds—sedatives, antibiotics, pain relievers, fever reducers—then changed them when Josh couldn't tolerate them. His temperature would elevate unexpectedly, then be under control again. On Friday, February 14, Joe wrote:

Well, Josh, you had a great night. They changed your ventilator last night and you have been sleeping so well they dropped off giving you Ativan every two hours...Josh, you had a great day today...all your numbers looked good and you seemed as comfortable as you could be...your fever dropped around five this evening and you only needed Ativan once every four hours...today when you were awake, the nurse asked you to move your foot and you did...you were awake a lot longer today and you were more fired up…We have about two feet of snow and they are calling it a blizzard with wind and cold…they went up on your fentanyl 7.0 because they thought you were in pain but I think it is more anxiety…great morning without fever…Mom arrived about noon and she will be staying with you for the next couple of days…your intestines are starting to get better…all of your counts were perfect and the report with the morning team seemed very positive.

The doctors decided to try "sprint weaning" Josh off the respirator on Wednesday, February 19th, 18 days after he was admitted to CHOP. The first attempt was successful and many of his meds were reduced or discontinued at this point. Joe's relief is almost palpable throughout the next few journal entries.

Today is looking good. The MRI looks great and the spinal fluid shows no white cells. This is very good news. You had a great night and so far this morning you seemed comfortable…your color is good and your heart rate is staying between 137 and 150. A couple of times today they will be doing the sprint workout again to work towards getting you off the respirator. Just think of them as the ones your dad makes you do in basketball practice, and I am sure you will blow through these and move onto getting out of here. More good news today, nothing showed up in your cultures and you no longer have the RSV virus. But you are still fighting fevers. They will be doing a CT scan to see what is going on inside your stomach.

On Wednesday, February 26th, Joe wrote:

Today is a big day, Josh. They may take the tube out of your mouth.

And on the same day, he continued:

Well, they tore our hearts out today. The doctor said you were not ready because you were flaring your nostrils a little too much and working too hard to breath. So they are keeping the ventilator in.

The next day:

Today is HUGE…the tube is coming out…

And later:

All went well with the tube coming out, but man, were you mad, punching and grinding your teeth at me. I am sure you had a few choice curse words for me, too, but I could not understand them because your mouth is so sore.

On Friday, February 28th, Joe records:

> Today was a good day, but you were sedated a lot. Now the big step is to wean you off all the meds you have been on for the past weeks. You are on Fentanyl 10 mg. Valium and Pentobarbital. Today you were out of it a lot and did a lot of staring, but all that will change as they wean you off the meds.

The last entry is on Saturday, March 1st:

> Well, you had a great night. You slept most of the night. They want to give you a rest because you did so well, so they are going to keep you the same [on the same medications] but drop down on the Fentanyl to 9.5 mg.

All day on Saturday, Joshua stared out the window of his hospital room. He wasn't as agitated as he had been throughout the previous weeks. He was very quiet.

Saturday night there was a hemorrhage on his brain. He was taken in for surgery and was in the operating room for several hours. On Sunday, they kept trying to awaken him, and he would look at his mother, but without responding.

On Monday, Joshua Joseph Wilker—the sports-playing, rain-loving, rosary-praying boy with beautiful brown curly hair, a sweet round face, an unshakable love of God, and indomitable spirit—had a seizure.

The doctors told Rose and Joe that he would not recover.

Chapter Five

Although Joshua was considered legally dead on Monday, for the family's sake they waited until everyone could come to the hospital and have a chance to see Josh again before turning off life support.

Before everyone arrived, Joe carefully dressed Josh in his basketball jersey—Number 11—a medal that had been blessed by Mother Teresa, and his cross and rosary ring, which Josh always wore. When everyone was there, Joe's sister put black rosary beads, which were on the bed by his side, around his right hand. Since Sunday, Joshua had had no neurological or physical movement. The family stayed in the room for a little while, and then, when they were leaving, Rosemary's mother looked back at Josh and asked, "What happened to the rosary beads?" Rose looked down at his hand, and it was clutched shut with the beads totally inside his fist and just a part of the crucifix hanging out. She thought it was odd, but didn't say anything. She walked her mother out of the room and then returned. Joe had not left Joshua's side; yet, when Rose returned, Joshua's hand was now on his chest and Joe said he didn't move him nor did he see any movement. The ICU doctor was in the room with them, preparing to turn off life support.

Joe's closest friends kept vigil outside Joshua's hospital room door, their family doctor, J.T. Kane, and his brother Billy. Just then, a priest moved quietly from out of nowhere down the hall past the Kanes, then turned back toward them. He was holding a black prayer book straight out and with his thumb resting on top of its cover. He seemed to be searching and walked up to Rose who was standing in the doorway.

"Are you looking for Joshua Wilker?" she asked him.

He told her no and mentioned another name which she can't remember, but she does remember it was a very biblical sounding name. Then he asked if he could go in to pray for Joshua, and she brought him into the room where Joe and the doctor were standing beside Josh's bed. The priest, a thin older man with white hair dressed all in black, blessed Joshua and administered the Sacrament of the Sick. Afterward, Rose led him toward the door and he said to her, "We just want you to know we are praying for you and your family and never be afraid to ask a priest for help."

In Rose's words, "Suddenly, the priest just wasn't there anymore. He just sort of vanished."

J. T. said, "Where did he come from…or more to the point, where did he go?"

This was to be the first of many extraordinary occurrences and coincidences after Josh's death.

Josh was buried with his rosary ring and the rosary beads he had with him in the hospital. Joe and Rosemary wanted to keep his crucifix, and the funeral director removed the cross and gave it to them before closing the casket in which he left everything else.

Joshua was buried in a section of the cemetery beneath a small grassy hill where only one other grave was located. On the hill, Rosemary noticed a tall gray pillar. She was to find out later that Joshua's grave is near where all the Grey Nuns of the Sacred Heart are buried. Although there are no stones marking the sisters' graves, the pillar with the likeness of St. Marguerite D'Youville, the Grey Nuns' foundress, sits on the hill above Joshua's grave. (Coincidentally, Josh was born on the first day of his father's employment as a teacher at Grey Nun Academy, and Josh's baptismal day was on the feast of St. Marguerite D'Youville.) Rosemary received great comfort from knowing Josh's grave is near the sisters, although it was not planned, and she felt that her precious son was in good company and the sisters would watch over him.

At home later, Rosemary was showing someone a letter that had been sent to them before Josh's death. It was from a friend, Father Cassal, who lived in New York. He told them that he was saying mass for Josh on Sunday (which turned out to be the day Joshua had the brain hemorrhage). In the letter, he had advised them to pray that day only to Father Mychal F. Judge, the chaplain who on September 11 died with the first responders at the World Trade Center.

When Rosemary was putting the letter into a box where they were keeping things from the hospital, the black rosary beads—the very same rosaries that were buried with Joshua—were sitting on top of the other items. They had not been there the day before.

Rosemary knew without any doubt that she had given those beads to the funeral director along with Joshua's clothing, and he had placed them on Josh's hands. The beads were in the coffin with Joshua's body when the lid was closed.

"I was in shock. I am still in shock years later. We left them with him, yet here they were in the box. Can this really happen?"

As I said before, parents will grasp at any incidences they think connect them to their children who have died. Many people do it when a loved one goes before they do. And it is very difficult for others to believe that occurrences like these are real and not just coincidence, that events are supernatural—in fact, miraculous. For the most part, human beings are very skeptical—yet in many ways people are also superstitious. If something happens to us, we believe, but when it happens to others, we wonder if it could be true or deny it outright.

A few days later on March 11, struggling with the loss of her son, Rosemary went into his room. She spoke to him aloud. She opened her broken heart to him. She pleaded with him to help her through the pain and grief. She begged him for strength.

But grief is not fleeting, and a parent's grief is a life sentence. No great comfort for this heart-broken mother was forthcoming in that room.

She eventually left his room and walked to her own bedroom. There on the floor was a daily devotion book that contained a Scripture reading and below it a reflection by a guest author for each day. A neighbor had given it to Josh while he was ill and couldn't attend Mass. It hadn't been there earlier when she left her bedroom.

She picked it up and opened it to March 11. The reflection for that day read:

Running in the Rain,
from the Rain,
to the Rain
by Fr. James Stephen Behrens

For as the rain and the snow come down from heaven,
and do not return there until they have watered the earth,
making it bring forth and sprout,
giving seed to the sower and bread to the eater,
so shall my word be that goes out from my mouth;
it shall not return to me empty,
but it shall accomplish that which I purpose,
and succeed in the thing for which I sent it.
For you shall go out in joy, and be led back in peace;
the mountains and the hills before you shall burst into song,
and all the trees of the field shall clap their hands.
Instead of the thorn shall come up the cypress;
instead of the brier shall come up the myrtle;
and it shall be to the LORD for a memorial,
for an everlasting sign that shall not be cut off.
- Isaiah, Chapter 55

I love listening to the rain. It comes and yet there is more than sound to it. There is power in those trillions of drops. The earth absorbs the rain and from that there is abundant growth. Rain sustains life. Rain sustains us. We would die without rain.

We use umbrellas to keep us from getting wet. We devise all sorts of ways to keep the rain at bay. I remember seeing a little boy running in the rain. He laughed as he ran and had his mouth open and his tongue out. He did not mind getting wet. In fact, he seemed to love it. He ran and ran through it, his mouth wide open, drinking the rain and laughing.

Isaiah writes of rain as the power and love of God. There is a purpose to God's rain, God's love. Of course that little boy was too young to make such connections between Isaiah's words and love and rain and God. He is older now, and probably carries an umbrella. I hope he is safe from rain - the kind that makes him wet - but not the rain of Isaiah. I hope he loves that kind of rain and runs through it.

For we hide from love, for love can hurt us. If it rains real hard, when love comes to us hard and real, we even close our eyes because it hurts. If we are frightened, we may even cry tears from the rain that flows through our bodies.

Love asks a lot of us. We have all sorts of umbrellas to protect us from the exacting demands of love. Yet, love is the one thing in life that we can trust, for love is from God and there is a purpose to it. We do not always see that, and so we shield ourselves. But God still sends the rain, still sends his love. If we knew what it was that God sends us, we would run through it with each other and laugh and drink all the way. We would love getting drenched. Saints and little boys are wise enough to run through it with joy. I want to learn from them. I like to think that there will come a time when we will all laugh and run in the rain, the rain of God's love, and throw away forever everything we may have used to shield ourselves from God.

I do not know if Paradise has weather. I suspect there is a Wind. And I would guess there are no umbrellas but I would bet there is a special kind of rain, rain that tastes good and brings joy - the kind you want to run through. When I get to heaven, I will see all those I have loved and they will be soaking wet and laughing and running, running toward me, and will hold me in their arms and I will feel the wetness of God's love and the hot wetness of their tears. And they will love me into a life that is new but somehow familiar - familiar because of the rain that came to me from the time I first opened my mouth and cried for the milk of my mother's rain and my family's love. And I will remember with joy those times I was not afraid in life of the rain that pelted me every day and when I had, at times, the courage to taste it a bit, and then run, run, run - for it was God on the far side of that crazy storm, drenching me with the rain of his love as I ran toward him.[1]

As far as Rosemary is concerned, this was nothing less than a gift from Joshua to her and Joe and their other children. This passage was telling her that as devastated and grief-stricken as she was, she couldn't shut down, she couldn't stop loving. She had two young children who needed her and a husband who was just as grief-stricken and filled with pain as she was and who needed her. She didn't care if she sounded crazy now. Rosemary believed from that moment on Josh was working miracles, and she wasn't going to keep it a secret. There had to be a reason for Joshua's life, and if he continued to send her signs like these, she would make sure others knew about it.

From here on, the memory of Joshua would not be about death and pain or suffering—his or theirs.

His memory would instead bring love and comfort, and she knew that it wouldn't be just for the Wilker family and friends, but for anyone who needed to know that there is a *beyond*—a bigger and better beyond than we can ever imagine.

She knew clearly now that on the other side of death was life, and it was so close that even her young son's spirit could reach over this threshold to connect with and comfort them. And even though the earthly "rain" was pelting them right now, God's "rain of love" would soak them through to their hearts and souls with comfort.

Chapter Six

The thought of losing a child is always unbearable, yet parents do bear it. Losing a child can never be explained away with trite expressions or reasons, so parents don't usually try to reason why. They get up in the morning, eat, speak when they have to, get through the day, perform whatever tasks and chores are at hand, take care of their living children, and, for want of a better word, live. Sometimes they have to remind themselves to breathe because losing a child will literally take their breath away for long moments at a time. A huge piece of who they are is gone. They feel that a part of their bodies and chunks of their souls have been ripped away, and for a while, a long while—sometimes forever—they bleed the invisible blood that had sustained their joy on earth before the death of their child.

When they see signs—or even what could be thought of as miracles—it's natural for them and others to think that they are just searching for comfort, that they are grasping for connections to their beloved. Maybe that's all it is in the end. Yet, maybe it is more.

How many times have we heard stories about the living receiving strange messages and signs from the dead? There are professionals in the scientific world who have dedicated their careers to either prove or disprove these types of phenomena or happenings. Whole departments of universities around the world are devoted to the study of afterlife. Physicians around the world who are trained to treat patients strictly through medical science report "otherworld" phenomena.

There are no shortages of symbols—rainbows, butterflies, the scent of perfume or cigar out of nowhere, static from radios or phones, lights turning on or off. Numerous stories about the dead reaching out to contact the living are widespread, and some have a very common theme. Of course, there are people who will always come up with a reasonable or scientific explanation for these signs. But sometimes—perhaps more often than not—there just isn't any plausible reason, and explaining away the inexplicable is impossible even for the most skeptical.

The Roman Catholic Church is very careful about its position on signs from the afterlife. The Church doesn't reject it, but Church scholars are not quick to confirm it either. Yet, the Church doesn't proclaim it to be heresy if a person says that they have received a sign from a loved one who is dead. The Church does caution against séances or any act that could be contrary to the virtue of religion, and to attempt to see a loved one through a medium isn't acceptable, nor is it appropriate to try to seek the future and not let God unfold what is ahead for us in His own time.

Page Zyromski who writes for AmericanCatholic.org, published an article titled, "Witches, Ghosts and Magic: What Catholics Believe." In it, she asks the question, "Does the Church think there are ever people who can see the future for real?" And she answers, "Yes, says the Church. Our tradition is full of prophets and saints who have seen the future. This didn't stop when the last ink dried on the Bible."

She relates ESP experiences by Saints Benedict and John Bosco, among others, and she tells us, "It's not uncommon to hear an ESP story about the death of a loved one. Love is stronger than death, the Bible tells us. My son, for example, knew exactly when his grandfather died even though he was 500 miles away. It's important not to stretch the truth if this happens to you. Pray for your loved one and don't be afraid." [2]

The Catholic Church believes that the soul lives forever. The Communion of Saints—official and ordinary—is one of the most important teachings of the Church. To die is to live—we are not dying, we are entering life, and Catholics believe that our immortal souls will be reunited with our mortal bodies on the last day.

Catholics are not alone in this belief. Most Protestant denominations also believe this.

Jews also believe in an afterlife. In a sermon given by Rabbi Samuel Stahl in 2003, he answers the question, "Why don't Jews believe in an afterlife?"

"After the Bible was completed and canonized, Jews began to develop three different ideas of what happens to us after we die. First, to this day Orthodox Jews believe in the actual resurrection of the dead. At the end of time, when the Messiah comes, the dead will be assembled from the entire world and they will be raised from the dead near the Temple Mount in Jerusalem."

Rabbi Stahl goes on to tell us, "Those of us in the non-Orthodox community generally hold two other views of life after death. Few of us believe in resurrection. Rather we maintain that, after we die, the soul, the imperishable God-like part of us, will return to God. The body, on the other hand, will go back to the dust from which it originally came into life.

"In addition, we maintain that our beloved dead live on in the hearts and minds of their survivors. Our Gates of Prayer expresses this belief in these felicitous words: "By love are they remembered and in memory do they live." Thus, contrary to popular misconceptions, we Jews do cling to a notion that life does not end at the grave. Some Jews embrace a belief in the resurrection at the end of time. Others, especially in the Reform community, maintain that we live on perpetually through the immortality of our souls. We also remain alive as long as our influence will continue to be felt after our demise." [3]

Islam very strongly agrees in life after death. In a *Brief Guide to Understanding Islam*, the question of life after death is answered clearly.

"The question of whether there is life after death does not fall under the jurisdiction of science, as science is concerned only with classification and analysis of sense data. Moreover, man has been busy with scientific inquiries and research, in the modern sense of the term, only for the last few centuries, while he has been familiar with the concept of life after death since time immemorial.

"All the Prophets of God called their people to worship God and to believe in life after death. They laid so much emphasis on the belief in life after death that even a slight doubt in it meant denying God and made all other beliefs meaningless."

A *Brief Guide to Understanding Islam* continues, "The very fact that all the Prophets of God have dealt with this metaphysical question of life after death so confidently and so uniformly - the gap between their ages in some cases, being thousands of years - goes to prove that the source of their knowledge of life after death as proclaimed by them all, was the same, i.e. Divine revelation."[4]

So if many religions teach that souls continue into a new life after death, why not believe that they can contact us—leave us signs to comfort us, even protect us? First and foremost, we have to remember that only God is the author of our lives. He sends His angels to protect us, saints and prophets to guide us to goodness, but we must always receive this in the absence of evil, and with an open heart and mind that God's hand is in everything good that happens to us.

It may be true that some souls are a little stronger in death and more able to reach out to the living. Perhaps some of the living are a little more sensitive to recognizing signs and seeing the little miracles that happen to us from time to time. One person will see a rainbow after the death of a loved one and know in his or her heart that it is a sign. Another will just see a rainbow and chalk it up to the sun reflecting through moisture in the atmosphere. Does that mean it wasn't a sign, or just that the skeptic doesn't recognize it as such?

If we're open to the idea that we will live beyond life on earth, then isn't it feasible to think that we can still be somehow attached to those who are still on earth and reach out to them? And if we are able to imagine that, then wouldn't a young person's soul, a person who on earth was too young to really commit any grave sins and who suffered greatly before dying, be given the grace from God to send continuous comforting messages to those who are grieving for him or her?

The Wilkers believe it is so. Granted, some of the signs they have received are typical stories we've heard time and again, very coincidental. We can shrug and say, "Well, maybe…" Yet, some are inexplicable and more difficult to explain away.

Joshua's Ring

This is a photograph of Joshua taken not long before he died.

Below is a photograph taken at the scene of the Oakes' accident, which took place a few weeks after Joshua's death. The shadow of Joshua's head is visible above the car in which his classmate, Meredith, was critically injured and in a coma. Meredith was in a coma for several days, and immediately upon awakening, she related to her parents that Joshua appeared to her to tell her that it was not her time to die and asks her to tell his parents that he is alright and happy. Meredith, still recuperating from her injuries when this photo was sent to her mother for insurance purposes, immediately identifies Joshua's face in the photo.

No photograph in this book has been retouched or manipulated in any way except resized in order to fit the page. Some were digital photos and others have been scanned from the original print. This is from an original print. Please note that I have blown up the area of the photo that shows Joshua's face.

20

Joshua's Ring

In this photo taken at Joshua's grandmother's birthday party, his face can be seen in the window in the background.

Although difficult to see at first, the Wilkers' trained eyes can easily find the familiar impression of Joshua's face in this photo of Joe while vacationing in Colorado. Again, none of these photos have been retouched.

21

Joshua continues to be seen in some photos taken of his family members. Here his sweet face can be seen in the water where his brother Austin is preparing for crew practice. (Austin is behend the boy in the gold sweatshirt.)

His parents believe that through the unexpected white feathers they find and the image of his face in photographs like these, Joshua is reaffirming to them that there is life after death, and he is still near them and will be throughout their lives

Joshua with his little brother, Austin, and his baby sister, Erin.

CHAPTER SEVEN

It started with the priest who arrived unexpectedly and then disappeared, and it continued with the rosary beads that were buried with Joshua yet inexplicably were found in a box with his things. Then there was the daily reflections book Rosemary found on the floor of her bedroom on one of her darkest days in grief, with the reading for that particular day that presented a boy gleefully running in the rain—*God's rain of love.*

After Josh's death, Rose went to the shrine of St. John Neumann, a beloved Bishop of Philadelphia who was canonized a little more than 25 years ago. She always suspected that this saint, who loved children and established the Catholic school system in Philadelphia, may have been the spirit of the priest who had come to Joshua's dying bed. The images on prayer cards she'd seen looked a little like the priest, yet she couldn't be certain. At the shrine, she browsed in the museum at all the artifacts belonging to the Bishop. There on display was the prayer book, complete with a thumb print imbedded onto the cover, in exactly the way the priest who visited Joshua carried his prayer book. That was confirmation for Rose that something very spiritual was going on.

These incidences were only the beginning. More were frequent and poignant, and not only experienced by Rose but by others. Joe had a harder time seeing the signs, yet he wouldn't discount them.

Rose began a journal two months after Josh passed over to document the signs she and others were receiving. The first entry that mentions what she believed to be a message from Josh is on May 12, 2003.

    🌿 "Today I went to church and I saw someone there who had just found out about Josh. I became too upset and had to leave. I drove right to the grave to talk to Josh. It was a cloudy, windy day. When I got out to the site where Josh is buried, all of a sudden the sun became very bright and surrounded me with warmth. I thanked Josh and spoke to him. When I looked up into the sky, I saw a long straight cloud and another equally straight cloud looked as if it was being blown by a mouth-shaped cloud and it floated parallel to the first, which formed the number 11—the number Josh wore when playing sports. Usually when I talk to Josh, I see the number 11 somewhere."

    🌿 Later that month, one of Josh's classmates at Grey Nun Academy was in a very serious automobile accident. Rescuers had to use the Jaws of Life to remove Meredith and her mother, Susan, from the car. Meredith had to be revived by paramedics. She had a fractured skull, was rushed into surgery to remove skull fragments from her brain, and was kept in an induced coma to keep her from moving. When she did regain consciousness, one of the first things she said was that she had been with Josh, and he had told her it just wasn't time for her and that she had to return. He asked her to please tell his parents that he was all right. She did, almost immediately upon awakening from days of being unconscious. She spoke of Josh hovering over the car while the rescuers were trying to get them out. Meredith saw his face and he comforted her. She remembered a few days later that he also told her, "Don't focus on missing the body. Focus on the goodness."

A few months after the accident, while Meredith was still at home recuperating, her mother received photographs that were taken of the accident by a professional photographer. She left the photos on the kitchen table. When Meredith came into the kitchen, she looked down at them and immediately saw Josh's face as she had seen it when she was unconscious inside the car. She pointed it out to her mother, who could now see it as well. They gave the photograph to Rose and Joe.

Josh was in the eighth grade at GNA when he died. He was getting ready to graduate and move on to LaSalle High School where he had always wanted to go. He was excited about moving on, but a little sad, too. He had grown very close to his teachers and classmates, and as mentioned before, because of his sweet disposition and intelligence, he was a favorite among all of them.

At GNA, the teachers in the upper division (sixth through eighth grade) teach several subjects and the kids move from classroom to classroom as they would in a public junior high school. One of those teachers, Mrs. Myke Balough—an undisputed favorite among all the kids—teaches science, history, and religion. During the month of May that same year, she was teaching her sixth grade religion class about death. She compared going to heaven to human beings who were freed from slavery. After the class, she had a short break and went down to her mailbox which is near the administrative offices. In her mailbox was Josh's worksheet from when he was in the sixth grade—completed in his handwriting and with his name on it. It had not been there earlier when she checked the mailbox, and because it had been two years since he'd been in the sixth grade, she couldn't imagine where it came from. She was stunned. It was too much of a coincidence to be overlooked, and she told Rose and Joe about it.

When reading Rose's journal, it is evident that she was in great emotional pain, yet there is such hope in her writing, a resilience. She suffers from dark days, yet is able to pull herself out of the longing for her son to help others cope. Joe, too, although coping in a different way, did not close himself up completely as so many parents would after going through what they had gone through.

Every day he went to the school and was surrounded by children. Just months before, his son was among them, and we can only imagine what it is like to be in a sea of faces of children knowing the one face he wanted to see more than any other was not there.

Yet, he continued to coach, continued to guide these kids, deal with their little squabbles, their skinned knees, their wounded feelings.

Joe is a favorite teacher at GNA. The boys love him, the girls adore him, the other teachers are crazy about him, and the parents think he's the best. He knows kids and he never takes them too seriously—nor does he take the parents too seriously, either. He's down to earth, tough when he needs to be, and a softie the rest of the time. As a parent who had two children who were taught and coached in basketball by Joe, I know that he taught them that is isn't all about winning but that it really is how you play the game. Don't misunderstand—he wants to win, and he pushes them hard to be the best that they can be—in gym, in academics, on the playing field, and on the basketball court. But it is always with a spirit of fair play and decency. My own children are better adults because of his influence. Every year at the Christmas show, alumni flock to him—whether it's been a year since they graduated or ten years. He's their man. And the kids take his wisdom and guidance with them when they leave the doors of GNA. Mention the school to kids who graduated from GNA and his is the first name that comes up.

When Joshua died, Joe didn't see signs. In her journal, Rose agonized over Joe. "I'm trying to make more time with Erin and Austin. I need also to focus on Joe. He needs as much attention if not more. His sadness is just as strong as mine. He and Josh were buddies. Their bonding was starting to get stronger in Josh's teenage years, and they did everything together."

Rose knew Joe was extremely angry inside. She prayed almost daily that Joe would experience some sort of communication from Josh, but she also knew she couldn't push it. It wasn't that he didn't believe that others were seeing these signs, but he didn't see any.

Then, one Sunday in June, Joe went to Mass alone early in the morning and visited Josh's grave afterward. He stayed awhile, pining for his son, and then got into his van. As soon as Joe started the car, a song began to play on the radio station Joe listens to. It was Buddy Jewell's ***Help Pour Out the Rain*** (Lacey's Song). The lyrics are so important to this story, however, we were unable to obtain permission to use them. Briefly, the song talks about a man riding in his car with his little girl. The child begins to ask questions about heaven, and asks her father, "and do you think that God could use another Angel to help pour out the rain?"[5]

Joe sat in his car and listened to the song in its entirety. He finally had his sign.

After Josh's death, the family began to notice that whenever a photo was taken of one of them, a halo was evident somewhere in the photo. Sometimes it is bright, sometimes very light, but it shows up on almost all the early photos taken by different cameras and different people after Josh died.

In the summer of 2003, while at the New Jersey shore, a place that Joshua loved to be, Rose's mother brought along her camera, and once again there were halos in two of the photos. One was taken of her mother, and the halo actually looks as though it is moving toward her.

There is another photo of Erin in a tree, taken with a different camera, and the halo is three dimensional. In it, there is a boy playing with a dog.

Still other photos taken after Josh's death show a face, his face, somewhere in the composition similar to the one in the photo taken at Meredith's accident scene. Admittedly, they aren't easy to see at first without a trained eye, but once pointed out, the faces in the photos are very clear and very similar—eyes, nose, mouth, shape of head—always the same. Rose and Joe have come to know exactly what to look for, and sure enough, even years later, they are finding his face in photos taken of family members.

Other signs kept coming.

⤳ One afternoon in late summer the year Josh died, when Joe and Rose were out in their back yard, a neighbor they didn't know well and with whom they weren't close friends was weeding in her yard. Rose said to Joe, "I wish I knew that they had sports in heaven. Josh loved playing sports." As she finished saying it, the neighbor called over to them to tell them that she had found one of the kids' toys. Rose apologized and asked her to just throw it back over the fence into their yard, which the woman did. Rose went over to pick it up and couldn't believe her eyes. She writes in her journal:

> "I just filled up with tears and walked over to Joe. We had moved into our house in June of 1990. Josh turned two years old in September that same year. We had a huge party for his birthday. I gave all the boys these little Hallmark bears dressed up as football players as favors. This was one of those toys. It was dressed in a Philadelphia Eagles outfit. That had been thirteen years before and here it was in my hand in mint condition seconds after mentioning how much Josh loved sports. Thanks, Josh, I guess this is your way of telling us that there are sports in heaven. Once again he uses his cleverness to answer us."

The signs were becoming more frequent and stronger.

⤳ While still grieving for Josh, his older cousin went on vacation with her boyfriend. They were playing miniature golf, a favorite of Josh's, and she was thinking of him and missing him. She looked up and saw a heart and the name Josh carved in the bark of a tree near her.

⤳ Another cousin, Crystal, was talking on her cell phone with a friend. It was a philosophical conversation about whether they believed in life after death. Crystal was adamant that she believed. She told her friend about Josh and all the signs he'd been sending. Just then her room lit up bright and an old cell phone that had been out of service for a year and had not been charged for all that time started ringing. Crystal panicked, a little too "freaked out" to answer it, and grabbed the phone and ran to her mother with it. It stopped ringing, but when her mother looked at it, the time on the phone was 2:45. When these numbers are added together, they equal 11.

On Mother's Day weekend in 2004, more than a year after Josh had passed over, Rose and Joe agreed to let Austin move into Josh's room. Rose cleaned the room, took down curtains, vacuumed the ceiling and washed every inch of the wall and floors. She laundered the bedding and hung it outside to dry. She removed everything from the dressers and book shelves and dusted them.

She tackled the closet, organizing it, getting rid of what wasn't necessary. She found a large Rubbermaid container with crafts that Josh had made in school. She went through it carefully, looking at each creation, reading what he'd written, glad that she didn't get rid of anything. She found a little poem he'd written in first grade about a caterpillar who turned into a butterfly. At the end of the poem he had written, "And do you know who the butterfly is? It is me, myself." Even then Joshua had a sense of emerging from his body and being freed to turn into something even more beautiful than the human form.

She grew tired and was emotionally drained, and she told Austin they'd finish the job the next day. On Sunday, Mother's Day, she finished cleaning out the closet and then completely cleaned off the bookshelf in the room, making a pile with books that had been Joe's in college. She brought the books down to Joe to tell him that a local store was having a used book sale. He took them and told her he'd bring them over to the store. When she returned to the room, she saw that there was something on the same bookshelf that she had just left completely empty. It was a little gift Josh had made for her in Pre-K for Mother's Day eleven years earlier that was titled, "Someone's in the Kitchen."

Rose was overwhelmed. No one else was in the room, no one was even upstairs. This little gift had not been in the container in the closet that she'd looked through the night before. There just wasn't any reasonable explanation for this eleven-year-old Mother's Day gift to appear, except, as Rose believes, Josh left it for her.

She pulled herself together, as she always did, knowing that she had a family who needed her to be strong, and finished the room for Austin to move into the next day.

The next morning after everyone had left for school, she went back up into Josh's—now Austin's—room. She approached the bed and noticed a pile of what she at first thought was dirt on the floor. She wondered where it came from since she had scrubbed the room from top to bottom the day before. She bent to pick it up and froze. It was a pile of Josh's curls. "I just sat there in the middle of the floor, grasping them to my heart. I had chills all over my body."

On Joe's birthday, May 29, 2004, Joe's sister and brother-in-law planned a family outing to a Phillies game. Although Josh had been to games with his uncle and cousin, Austin and Erin had never gone before this. The whole family was excited and looking forward to going, and they were going to be sitting in a box at what was then the new stadium. It was a bright, sunny day, about sixty degrees. The view was perfect from that box.

Joe's brother Mike was seated against a brick wall that divided their box from the next one. He sat there the entire time, not moving, watching the game intently for about an hour. He stood suddenly, although there was a player at bat, and moved from the seat. The batter hit a foul ball, which drove back up to their box and smashed against the wall where Mike had just been leaning. Their nephew Christian bent down and picked it up and handed it to Austin, who was in his glory. They all looked down and the batter who had hit the foul ball was Number 11. "This was no coincidence," Rose writes in the journal. "It was Josh trying to let us know that he was with us. Thanks J-man for wishing your dad a happy birthday and letting us know you are always with us."

As time goes on, the Wilkers have learned to have some fun with Josh's signs and they find themselves laughing more now.

At a golf outing in honor of Josh in September of 2004, Joe's "five-some"—his brothers and nephew—were just about in last place. At the last hole, Joe hit what he was writing off as the worst shot of the day. The ball flew out towards the trees, hit a tree, dropped straight down and plunked right into the water, then popped out of the water, skidded up onto the green and stopped right next to the hole. Everyone who saw it exploded in laughter. Joe just looked up into the heavens and said, "Very funny, Josh! Why not put it in the hole for me?"

Joshua loves to leave white feathers, and does so frequently, not only for his parents but for others who have been thinking of him or praying for or to him.

One day a mother from the school was talking to Rose on the phone before school started. Joe and Austin were already at basketball practice, which Joe held before class began. The woman told Rose that her husband had a stroke, but that he was recovering at home. She mentioned that she was praying to Josh to intercede for her husband. They got into a discussion about signs, especially the ones that Josh had been leaving, and Rose told the woman about the white feathers he would leave from time to time. When they hung up, Rose realized she was late taking Erin to school and rushed out of the house. When she returned, there was voice mail from the woman to whom she'd spoken earlier. The woman, whose voice was very excited and close to tears, said in the message that immediately after their conversation, she hung up the phone, turned around and found a white feather on her table. She and her husband knew now that Josh was listening.

One snowy day, Rose's mother was on her way to the store. She had a bad case of the blues that day. A grandmother's love is very strong and very deep, and she was having an extremely difficult time dealing with Joshua's death as would be expected. Time wasn't easing her grief. And on that cold snowy day as she drove to the store she prayed to Josh. She told him she could really use a feather to get her through the sadness. Looking through her windshield at the swiftly falling snow, she thought to herself that she wouldn't be able to find it under all the snow even if he did send one. She arrived at the store and there on the ground as she entered the store was a yellow feather. "He likes to be funny," Rose explains in her journal.

⤸ March Madness in Bucks County is a basketball tournament involving the local private and Catholic schools in the area. It's one of the Wilkers' favorite times, although without Josh, March Madness has lost some of its luster. Yet Joe continues to organize and look forward to the tournament. When he sets up the gym for March Madness and puts out the chairs for the team, he always puts out an extra chair. It's a tradition now. The chair is for Joshua.

During March Madness of 2005, Joe lined up the chairs courtside, the kids came in, the game began, and Joe coached. The players moved up and down the court, the basketball was passed from hands to hands and into the net, they pivoted, they dribbled, they faked and fouled, they guarded and they rebounded. Joe ran along the sidelines with them, shouting out plays, calling his players by name, encouraging them—all the while, longing for his son Joshua, and picturing him out there on the court with his classmates. Amidst the excitement and pandemonium that a basketball game creates, Joe glanced over at the empty chair. There on the metal seat lay a fluffy white feather.

These signs—which Rose and Joe believe to be messages from Joshua—inspired Joe to write a thank you letter to everyone who had been supportive of the Wilker family after Josh died. He entitled this letter "Signs" and wrote it as though it was from Joshua.

SIGNS

This letter is so overdue and so inadequate, but I want to express my true feelings toward all of you. I was hoping to tell you personally how much you have meant to me and my family, but as you know, I had another calling. I am back with my first father again and meeting some new family members and some old friends that I have missed for a while. Words cannot express what all of your generosity and support have meant to my mother, father, sister and brother. They still have their moments and will for a while, but like Jimmy Valvano*, The North Carolina State Basketball coach, every day you should cry, laugh, and think a little bit. He passed away shortly after winning the NCAA tournament, after being diagnosed with cancer.

I'm sorry that I haven't answered all of you, but I want you to know I hear you when you talk to me. I have been having a little fun since I left you and I have been doing a lot of traveling. You'd better believe I was in New Orleans on Fat Tuesday, eating some donuts and pancakes with ice cream (you never gain weight up here!), and of course I had to stay and watch the NCAA finals with J.T., Willy and his family in the box (I know what all of you did!).

I've been having fun with Mrs. Balogh when she thinks she is alone in the science lab at night (yes, Mrs. Balogh, that's me when you hear that strange noise and think that someone is with you). Please keep talking to me, Mrs. Balogh, I like that.

My mother has been seeing a lot of signs, but my father is not that good at it yet, but keep trying, Dad. My mother sees me a lot. At times, I leave feathers of my angel wings around when I am visiting her and she knows when I am walking with her side by side. I let her and Erin see me the other day in the clouds when they were coming from soccer, and yes that dog I was with was Zonka. I was there at the basketball tournament when Brian, Brennan, and Larry decided to shoot threes all game, just like me, but I usually make most of them. Thanks, Margretta, for giving me a seat to sit on at night. All this flying gets me tired at times.

I had a nice visit from Meredith the other day. You know Mer is always in a hurry to get to some place new, but I had to tell her it was not time yet, that we were not ready for her. She has something to finish before we meet again. But it was great to see her again. Thank you, Meredith, for delivering that message to my family. They really needed to know that I had arrived, and was happy and doing OK. Also, thanks for letting me earn my wings so fast.

I have to go now. Jimmy V is going to show me a couple more moves, and talk about standing room only!* Dad, wait till you see this stadium I'm playing in now, you will love it.

Again, I can't thank you enough for what you did for me when I was with you all, and how much love you are showering my family with. Please remember I can hear you all, and miss you all so very much, but I can do so much more up here to help all of you. Just please ask me, I would love to help everyone.

In closing I want to thank my classmates. I love you all and am with you on your journey through high school. It is time for fun now, and you'd better believe I will be with you in Hershey Park on June 1st.

Love Always,
Your angel J.J. Wilker

* Author's note: The year after he died, Joshua was honored at the local Second Annual Jimmy V Basketball Tournament for Cancer—all the proceeds go to the V Foundation for Cancer Research. The V Foundation was started in honor of Jim Valvano, the popular North Carolina State University basketball coach, who died of Metastatic Adenocarcinoma at the age of 47. He was one of Joshua's favorite basketball coaches.

Chapter Eight

And sometimes there is talk of miracles—or more accurately, the answer to prayers.

The last entry in Josh's journal, written two months before his last trip to the hospital, were three wishes: to be rich, to have super powers, to be cures for all sickness.

If all the signs he has sent to his parents and others are to be believed, then there's no disputing that Joshua Joseph Wilker now has super powers. Has he attained the status of being rich? We should never assume that someone goes to Heaven automatically, but it's hard to believe Josh isn't there, and if he is, then he knows riches we can't even imagine and can only hope we attain after our lives on earth are over.

But is he "cures for all sickness"?

At first, people prayed for Josh, the boy who was so sick and died too young. But shortly after his funeral, people started to pray *to* him, asking him to intercede for them. Rose purchased a bag of the rosary rings that Josh had worn while he was ill and that had given him great comfort. When someone was ill or troubled, Rose asked if they wanted a ring, and usually they did. They called them "Joshua's rings."

Rose was giving them out regularly—more than 1,000 have been dispensed. And, like Josh, many people have found comfort in having them. Some claim they have brought them miracles.

It is for the Roman Catholic Church to decide if the stories that are attributed to Joshua doing what most people would call "miracles" are in truth miraculous, and there is a lengthy process for that. Suspected miracles have to be documented, the people who claim to have been cured by the miracles have to be interviewed, doctors have to be interviewed, and that which is for the most part un-provable has to be proven.

"The required miracle must be proven through the appropriate canonical investigation, following a procedure analogous to that for heroic virtues."[6] In other words, the person whose soul is attributed to performing the miracle should have had Christian virtues considered heroic, that is, the theological virtues: faith, hope and charity, and the cardinal virtues: prudence, justice, temperance and fortitude, and others specific to his state in life.

Most Catholics pray *for* and sometimes *to* those who have passed into eternal life. The Catechism of the Catholic Church tells us, "In full consciousness of this communion with the whole Mystical Body of Jesus Christ, the Church in its pilgrim members, from the very earliest days of the Christian religion, has honored with great respect the memory of the dead; and 'because it is a holy and wholesome thought to pray for the dead that they may be loosed from their sins she offers her suffrages for them.' Our prayer for them is capable not only of helping them, but also of making their intercession for us effective."[7]

Joshua's Ring

It appears that Joshua's intercession for some people who prayed for his help has been effective.

    One woman, who was scheduled for eye surgery and was very nervous, prayed to Josh that the surgery would go well. In the hospital, she was prepped for surgery but immediately before being taken in for the procedure, the doctor checked the woman's eyes. This was not the first time he had seen her and examined her, but now he told her that she wasn't a candidate for this intricate surgery and that if he performed the surgery, she may become blind. He cancelled the surgery.

    Another woman, who the Wilkers didn't know, was suffering with a rare lung disorder that had compromised her immune system. She was very weak and couldn't eat. Her quality of life was diminished and her health had deteriorated to the point that she was no longer eligible to be on the list for a lung transplant. She was given just a few months to live. A friend of the Wilkers who knew this woman's daughter gave her one of Joshua's rings and told her to have her mother pray to Josh for intercession. After being given the ring, the woman started to eat again. She was able to get on the treadmill for short periods of time to strengthen her muscles. Within a short time, she was placed on the lung transplant list again.

    A young man who had also graduated from Grey Nun Academy several years before and who was diagnosed with ALL the same day that Josh was, continued to fight for his life. Joe and Rose prayed constantly for him. One Christmas Eve they were told that he had taken a turn for the worse. Rose prayed to Josh to intervene and ask God to help, if just to get him through the holidays. Weeks later, Joe met the boy and his mother at a local hardware store. He was out of the hospital and out and about. He did pass away late in January, but his family had him with them for the holidays.

    Rose's business associate's son was diagnosed with testicular cancer at the age of 24. Rose knew that her associate, Mike, was very angry and fearful. He told Rose that he had no confidence in the doctors and didn't believe them when they said the cure rate for this cancer was 95 percent. He knew that the doctors had told the Wilkers the same thing when Josh was first diagnosed, and this man just couldn't trust that his son would be all right. Rose tried to reassure him and told him to pray to Josh for help. She told him that Josh's signal was the number 11 or that he sometimes sent a feather as a sign.

On the day of the young man's surgery, his father and brother went to Johns Hopkins to be with him. When they got to the room, Mike stopped in his tracks. The room number was 11. In that moment he felt positive that his son would be all right. Indeed, one year later, his son called to say that he had his check up and the doctors told him he was cancer free—and he remains so today.

    In the month of July in 2005, Joe asked Rose to accompany him to Grey Nun Academy on the first day of All Ball Camp that is held at the school. She agreed, and when they got to the gym, she noticed that the large fans located on the stage were not on. She asked Joe about it and he told her they needed to be turned on because it keeps the kids cooler in the heat. She went up onto the stage to turn them on and an older man who was working at the camp followed her. She introduced herself and showed him how to turn the fans on and he thanked her.

When she was walking back to the door, he followed her and introduced himself as Jim O'Boyle, and asked her if the number 11 jersey that was hanging on the wall of the gym was her son's. He went on to mention that he had met Joe before and while in Joe's office, he saw the photos of Josh and learned about Josh's death. He wanted to tell her how sorry he was that she had lost her child. He had also lost a son from cancer seven years earlier. Rose recognized the pain in his eyes and the ache in his chest that she knew all too well. It was visible on his face.

They began to tell each other about their sons. They also exchanged episodes that had happened to them after their sons' deaths—signs as they called them. They were standing outside the gym and it began to rain lightly, yet they continued to talk, to share, all the while standing in the summer rainfall. Rose told Jim about how much Josh loved the rain and suggested laughingly that Josh and his son must be together, sending the rain down to them while they talked. She then told Jim about Josh's three last wishes and about the Rosary rings and the comfort people feel whenever she gives them out.

They finished talking and said goodbye to one another.

After the week-long camp, the Wilkers left for the shore for ten days. Going to the shore without Joshua never got any easier for Joe and Rose, the trips brought on very strong memories of what he loved and who he was. Rose writes in the journal:

> "It is by far the hardest place to be without Josh. One might think it gets easier to be there, but 95 percent of the time there I can think of nothing but Josh. How he loved the beach."

Yet they went with their families and friends every year, catering to their living children's needs, knowing that their lives had to go on. And although it brought so much sadness to them, being with those who loved them brought comfort, too.

> "How lucky we are to have such wonderful friends who welcome us like family to their shore homes," Rose writes in her journal. "If I can't say anything else, I must say that our family has been blessed with wonderful people and good friends, and Josh knew it. He had mentioned it in the autobiography he wrote for school before he died. I know he cherished every moment he had here on earth and lived life to the fullest."

And in her journal, Rose reminds herself often that just as Josh cherished life, she must do the same.

When they returned back from the shore vacation, she listened to their phone messages. One of them was from the son of the man she had met on the first day of All Ball Camp, Jim O'Boyle. All he said was that his father had told the family about Joshua's rings and they wondered if they could get some. Several messages after that there was one from Jim's wife, Tess, asking again for the rings.

Rose returned Tess's call. Tess explained to Rose that Jim had told her about their meeting, about Josh and the signs they had been receiving, and of course, about the rings. She went on to tell Rose that not two weeks after that chance meeting, Jim diagnosed with cancer and was hoping that he could have a ring. Rose sent them 11, then sent additional rings a week later because Tess wanted the entire family to have them.

Jim Boyle did not survive. His wife Tess wrote and thanked Rose for the rings. She said Jim was wearing the ring, it brought him comfort, and he was at peace when he died. Rose said, "My meeting him was definitely no coincidence. And I can remember standing in the rain talking, and he was so proud to be talking about his own son who he had lost to cancer. It is a day I will never forget...nor will I ever forget Jim."

In October of 2005, a friend of the Wilkers called Rose to ask for two rings. She had just found out that two of her friends were diagnosed with cancer—one with pancreatic cancer and the other with colon cancer. Rose mailed the rings to her immediately; however, when they were at a party of a mutual friend on a Saturday night several weeks later, the woman told Rose she never received them and she needed one immediately for one of her friends for Monday. Rose had some in her purse and gave them to her friend.

On Tuesday, Rose's friend called to say that one of the women who had received a ring had been told by physicians previously to get her affairs in order as there was nothing more they could do for her. She had seen five doctors and met with another one for more testing that Monday. The woman went to the physician's office and brought along her previous x-rays and reports.

After the follow-up tests that day, the new doctor could not find any cancer in her body. He could not explain why.

Sometimes miracles come in forms we don't recognize as miracles.

Throughout all of this grace that Rose and Joe felt they were receiving, they were after all still grieving parents.

Men and women have a tendency to deal with grief differently, which can often put couples at odds when they are both grieving. Chances are they feel the same emotions, but express it at different ends of the spectrum.

Reuters' studies have generally found that while bereavement brings some couples closer together, the general risk of divorce appears to climb after losing a child. The divorce rate among couples who report that the reason for their divorce is due to the death of a child is as high as 16 percent.

Rose and Joe Wilker are very normal, down-to-earth people, and although their faith is very strong, they are prone to the challenges and trials that grief always presents. And after Josh's death, although still deeply in love with one another, they were also very unhappy. Even a year later, Rose couldn't understand Joe's constant anger with her and with their other children, and writes in her journal:

> "Well Easter is upon us. The anniversary of Josh's death has come and gone and things are still rough between Joe and myself. Something has got to be done. The pain of the loss is not getting easier. I just keep letting Josh be with me, and I keep asking God to somehow intervene and make things better. We need to start talking. I cannot take the way we are treating each other. We use to have an occasional bad day or two, but nothing like this.
>
> "It is Easter morning and although we are acting happy for the kids, the tension is still thick. Joe decided he was not going to my parents as we planned."

In *Swallowed by a Snake: The Gift of the Masculine Side of Healing,* Tom Golden, a speaker, author, and psychotherapist whose area of specialization is healing from loss and trauma, states:

> "The expression of anger seems more natural for men than expressing other feelings. When expressing anger, we need to take a stand, to define our ground. This is quite different from the mechanics of sadness, which require a more open and vulnerable stance. It is important to note that men in our culture will sometimes find their other feelings of grief through their anger. Many times in working with men I have found that while a man is expressing anger (and I mean really expressing it.....loudly, with movement of the body, etc.), he suddenly will be moved to tears. It is almost as if touching on that profound and deep feeling of anger has brought him in touch with his other feelings. This process is reversed with women. Many times a woman would be in tears, crying and crying. I might ask what her tears are about, and she often would state plainly and many times loudly 'I'm angry.'
>
> "A person's anger during grief can range from being angry with the person who died to being angry with God, and all points in between."[9]

Those points in between can be each other, and even without knowing it, a very loving couple can push each other away because of their grief. Joe's anger—even hostility at times—was obvious and disheartening for Rose.

Shortly after Rose's initial passage about their problems on Easter, she writes in her journal:

> "Things came to a head. We started fighting. And finally I say, "You know, I

miss him too!" And we start apologizing to each other and start getting every-thing out. I was like a volcano that just exploded. I started saying everything that was bothering me and all the horrible things he was doing and saying. I couldn't stop. I must have rattled on for 30 minutes. I do not even think he realized what he was saying. I, of course, was not better. I wasn't treating him any better.

"Oh my gosh, what relief. It was all out in the open. My goodness, this feels great; it hasn't lessened any of the hurt of losing Josh, but we finally realize we were both so overwhelmed with the loss that we were venting our anger in the wrong way.

"We all did celebrate Easter at my parents and things are much better. All I can say is thank you, thank you to God, thank you to Josh and thank you to Joe. Let's put this horrible way of treating each other and everyone around us in the past and let Josh be with us in the spiritual form as he is trying to show us. I think sometimes we need to just sit still and be quite and just listen and feel. And use our sixth sense…It is so peaceful to just do that and feel the person you are missing. I think they are just right here, so perfect and so pure and without all the bodily feelings, physically and mentally."

Joe and Rose continue to have issues from time to time; every year is filled with poignant reminders—Josh's birthday, the anniversary of his death, the holidays, Mother's Day, Father's Day, March Madness, days at the Jersey shore—and these reminders always bring a pang of longing for the boy who died too young. Yet because of the signs they've received from him, they know that Josh is there, guiding them back to one another. And he never misses an opportunity to send them a feather to remind them…even when they least expect it.

Several years after Josh's death, Rose writes in her journal:

This morning Joe got us all up and started breakfast. Erin came down first and started eating. Austin was in the shower and I came downstairs. At this point Joe and Erin were outside and were coming back in the house. Joe said to me, "Your son is here today."

Joe had been outside drinking his coffee looking up in the sky when Erin came out and asked him what he was doing? He told her he was saying good morning to her brother Josh. Just as he said that, a flash of white came dropping from the sky and hit the ground. He said to Erin, "Great, a bird just crapped on us!" Erin started laughing and picked up the projectile from the sky; it was a white feather. It had come down so fast and hard that Joe didn't recognize it was a feather. So it was a hello from heaven. As always, thanks for staying connected. I wonder what Josh is up to. When we start getting a lot of feathers and signs, he is usually preparing us for something good or for someone leaving us and going to heaven. In any case I am so glad he stays in touch.

In 2009, the child of close friends of the Wilkers died. She was a young girl, full of promise, beautiful. Her name was Leah. Rose and Joe's heart went out to her parents. They know what it is like to face this profound sadness, this grief of burying a child, even though they feel that the separation is not much more than a gentle veil between earth and where their beloved has gone.

Two months before Leah died, her uncle wrote a beautiful note to her that has brought great comfort to not only Leah's family, but to the Wilkers as well. Sometimes when we see a person we love suffering, we wonder if it wouldn't have been better if that person had never been born. It's a normal reaction. It's just too painful to think we're going to lose that beloved person. This note addresses that. In part, it reads:

LEAH'S LEGACY

Leah,

I told your parents a couple of months ago that I went to confession because I was so mad at God for making you suffer. The priest was a very old and gentle man. He said, "Sorry, God doesn't work that way. He doesn't give this one dandruff, this one cancer, and that one a heart attack."

He put it to me this way: He said, "If God came to you and asked you if you would accept a gift from Him, what would you say?" He continued, "This gift would be the gift of a beautiful little girl, who will bring you smiles, laughter, tears, joy, and teach you so much about love and life that your mind can't begin to imagine the possibilities."

The priest then said, "There's a catch; you may only have her for a short time, but remember, she will bring you all of these gifts along with lessons of sacrifice and love."

Father said, "Would you accept this gift? Most people would."

The answer would be yes, for no matter how long we have a person we love, that person has put an indelible mark on our hearts and souls and is bound to us forever. God intended for that person to be in our lives, no matter if it was for a few moments, a year, a decade, or a generation. Love is too important for us to wish it away because it may have been painful to lose.

Chapter Nine

Rose writes in her journal:

> "I know that we do not always get the miracle we are praying for, but sometimes we don't realize that most of the time we pray for the wrong things and for the wrong reasons. I believe one day when we are no longer here on earth, we will realize that the real miracle we want is entering into heaven. Most of the time we are unaware that we are praying for the wrong kind of miracle."

Rose and Joe Wilker believe their son is in Heaven and they also believe that he has been communicating with them through signs. They also believe that the prayers of people who ask for his intercession are being answered in some way.

They want other people who are grieving to know that death is not the end; it is the beginning of something bigger and better. Our souls triumph over our bodies' death.

Like the ring that Joshua wore, the life of our soul is a circle—there is no end—it begins with God and stays with Him. That is what they believe God is allowing Josh to tell them.

Time doesn't ease the pain. As stated before, losing a child is a life sentence for a parent. But the Wilkers believe that knowing that there is something greater beyond this life, and that some souls that have entered into eternal life may reach out to the grieving on earth, is an enormous comfort.

Their concern in conveying this message, however, is that others who may not be experiencing signs or answers to prayers from loved ones who have passed on will feel hurt—even angry—after reading this. They shouldn't feel that way.

Just as people have different paths to follow in life on earth, souls may have different roles to play in eternal life. There is no way for us to know God's plan for us in either place.

God truly does work in mysterious ways and it is for us to trust in His ways, even those that are difficult to accept and understand. The Wilkers and their family are a model for all of us in accepting God's mysterious ways with grace and faith.

Joshua's Ring

Epilogue

This excerpt of a letter from Rose to Brother James Rieck, Director of Admissions at LaSalle High School, the school that Joshua had been planning to attend before he became ill, is a beautiful tribute to her son. LaSalle had accepted Joshua into their freshman class for the fall of 2003, which thrilled Josh and was something that brightened his days during his illness. Although Joshua died before he could attend the high school he longed to attend, LaSalle honored Joshua during those four years and at the graduation of the Class of 2007.

March 31, 2003
Dear Brother James,

I am writing to thank you for coming to the service for Josh. I also want to thank you and your staff for accommodating us while Josh was sick and for the card you sent us along with the retreat, and the many times you have mentioned and prayed for Josh at LaSalle. This was one of his biggest goals, to go to La-Salle. It gives us such comfort knowing that he knew he achieved this before he joined God and that you will remember him as part of the Class of 2007.

Since the service for Josh, we have experienced many unbelievable things that I would like to share with you so that you will really come to know Josh…

Here Rose relates to Brother James all the miraculous signs the family experience. She goes on to write:

I always knew Josh was a special child. As Joe said at his funeral Mass, from the time he was little he always spoke of going to heaven; he couldn't wait to get to heaven. He said this many times throughout his short life, never ever being afraid. He lived a very full and rewarding life, getting to do things that many people will never get to do in this lifetime and was always thankful and considered himself lucky.

Even after the first time he was in the hospital, and we were riding in the car, he said to me he couldn't believe how so many people were being so nice to him and sending him all kinds of nice things. He said he wanted to have a big pizza and hoagie party when he got back to school for everyone because they were so nice to him and he wanted to do something nice for all of them.

I now know that Josh was sent to all of us to remind us of what our goal in life is and what is important. We spend so much time worrying about things that really do not matter. I am truly saddened by the loss of my best buddy, but I know that if things were the other way around, and it was me who was gone and Josh was left here, he would not be sad. He would consider me the lucky one and would be truly happy that I was in Heaven.

On one final note, we know besides going to Heaven, that Josh's other big goal was going to LaSalle. When Josh was three, my nephew who was 21 at the time, stayed with us for the summer. He became very close to Josh and when Josh was five, Craig came back and stayed with us in the fall for about two weeks while debating what he wanted to do with the rest of his life. Craig brought his video camera with him and most of the time he was here, all he did was video Josh. He left a copy of it with us when he came back for Josh's funeral. It was entitled Philadelphia 1995. At the time Joe was coaching football for Bishop Egan High School. Craig's video was of us at the game and how ironic, Egan was playing LaSalle High School. There was Josh, at one of LaSalle's football games!

I feel that Grey Nun Academy, praying the Rosary, and LaSalle High School have all been a part of his whole life here on earth. Maybe he is a saint of the new millennium.

There are many other events that have happened, and he touched so many people. I know he will be roaming the halls of LaSalle High School come fall.

Thank you again for honoring Josh at your school. I hope you get a chance to read what he wrote about himself. He was quite a remarkable kid and we were lucky, because he was ours to share with the rest of the world.

"He will swallow up death

in victory:

and the Lord God will wipe away tears

from off faces…"

Isaiah 25:8

CHRONOLOGY OF SOME OF JOSHUA'S MESSAGES

March 4, 2003	Although Joshua had been declared brain dead for more than 24 hours, the rosary beads that had been draped over his hands in his hospital bed were inexplicably found in Joshua's fist. Joe was with him the entire time and no one had moved or touched Joshua.
March 4, 2003	The day that life support was being removed from Josh, a mysterious priest appeared at the hospital room door, came in and prayed over Josh. The priest told them, "We are praying for you and your family and don't ever be afraid to ask a priest for help." And then he was gone – just disappeared. Rose later realized—through photographs and at the Shrine of St. John Newman—that the saint was the priest who visited them that day.
March 7, 2003	A friend who was planning to purchase vestments in memory of Joshua dreams about a chalice and paten sitting on the altar of the Chapel at Grey Nun Academy—the chalice is scratched. When she goes to the store the next day to buy the vestments, the exact chalice with the scratch and paten were in a display case. She purchased them along with the vestments feeling that Joshua was somehow attached to the dream she'd had.
March 11, 2003	On a particularly difficult day of grieving, Rose found a *Daily Reflections Book* in her bedroom that had not been there earlier. It had belonged to Josh. She opened to the date, and there she found a passage about God's Love and the rain, and how saints and little boys run through it with joy. This proved to her that Joshua was communicating and comforting her.
March 12, 2003	Rose found the rosary beads that were buried with Josh in a box in their home.
March 2003	Immediately after an automobile accident in which Josh's classmate Meredith Oakes was seriously injured and left in a coma, Joshua greets Meredith and tells her it isn't her time to die, and that when she awakens, she must tell his parents that he is alright. Meredith was in a coma for several days, but that is the only "dream" she had during that time.

June 2003	Grey Nun Academy teacher, Myke Balogh, found an essay in her school mailbox that Josh had written when he was in the sixth grade two years before his death—it is his essay about life after death which she taught only a few minutes earlier that day to the sixth grade students
Summer 2003	A photograph taken at the scene of the accident that almost took Meredith Oakes' life, showed a shadow of Joshua's face above the car. Meredith recognized it the minute she looked at the photograph. When Rosemary and Joe looked at it, they saw that his head is bald and the mark where he had the brain hemorrhage that took his life is evident in the shadowy image.
February 2004	More photographs taken at a family birthday party reveal Joshua's face.
May 2005	Rose's colleague's son was diagnosed with cancer and needed surgery, and while she comforted this man, she told him that her son's "special" number was 11 and tells him to pray to Joshua to intercede for his son. When he entered his son's hospital room, he saw that the room number was 11.
March 9, 2006	Joe found a white feather on an empty chair that was courtside during a March Madness basketball game, Joshua's favorite sports event of the year.
May 29, 2006	When Rose began to prepare the family's favorite dinner in celebration of Joe's birthday, there was a white feather sitting on top of the pot she always uses for that feast.
November 2005	Wilkers visited family in Colorado and two photos taken of Joe reveal an image of Joshua's face in the grass.
February 2009	In a photo taken on Austin's first day of practice for LaSalle's crew team, Josh's face is reflected in the water near Austin.

Joshua's Ring

Endnotes

1 Behrens, Fr. James Stephen. "Running in the Rain, from the Rain, to the Rain." Living Faith, Volume 18, Number 4, James E. Adams Editor, Mark Nilesen Associate Editor. Canada: Creative Communications for the Parish, January-February-March 2003

2 Zyromski, Page. "Witches, Ghosts and Magic. What Catholics Believe." American Catholic.org, October 2001. http://www.americancatholic.org/newsletters/yu/ay1001.asp (September 2009)

3 Stahl, Rabbi Samuel M. "Three questions Christians ask of Jews." Beth-Elsa. org, May 3, 2002. http://www.beth-elsa.org/be_s0503.htm (October 15, 2009)

4 World Assembly of Muslim Youth. "How Do Muslims View Death? A Brief Illustrated Guide to Understanding Islam," No Date Listed. www.islam-guide.com/life-after-death-by-wamy.htm (October 15, 2009)

5 Jewell, Buddy. "Help Pour Out the Rain." *Buddy Jewell*. Neilson SoundScan 1990

6 Canonization Process. Catholic Pages.com, Vatican City, September 12, 1997. http://www.catholic-pages.com/saints/process.asp

7 Ibid

8 Libreria Editrice Vaticana, Catechism of the Catholic Church. Page 250, Number 958. 1994

9 Golden, Thomas R. Swallowed by the Snake, The Gift of the Masculine Side of Healing. Kensington, Maryland: Golden Healing Publishing, LLC 1996

Joshua's Ring

Afterword by Rosemary Wilker

I hope this book brings peace and comfort to all who read it.

This year is the Year of Faith in the Catholic Church, and it is the year that this book will be published. I guess that is what Josh was waiting for.

I would like to especially thank Cyndi Chapman who advised me to journal. I am so grateful for that bit of advice. Journaling helped me to cope with the loss of a remarkable kid, and it opened my eyes to eternal life. We are so involved with our own daily routines and families that we don't take the time to stop and feel the presence of our loved ones who we think are gone. In reality they are here guiding us on to the next journey in our life—hopefully to one that is more peaceful, full of only love and one that is forever.

Next, I'd like to thank our neighbor Maryellen who gave Joshua the Crucifix ring. He wore it from the moment she gave it to him and never took it off unless he had to for medical reasons. Maryellen and Josh always had a special bond and the ring was important to him.

Also, we owe so much to Brother James from LaSalle College High School. It was Brother James who pushed Joe to have us publish the incredible events that we are experiencing through Josh's spirit and he had a hand in getting us to publish. We are forever grateful. I am saddened to find out that Brother James, the man who took Josh under his wing even before he was accepted to LaSalle, has passed away. It was sudden.

Brother James made sure the school and those who would have been Josh's classmates knew about Josh and honored Josh's acceptance to LaSalle all 4 years, even though our son never had the opportunity to attend. He then spent these last 4 years molding and guiding Austin. He managed to be there all four years of Austin's high school experience. It has made him a remarkable kid and now one of the "Men of LaSalle". I am so thankful that my children and family were blessed to be part of the LaSalle experience. I have said many times that I love that school. If I could have sent Erin there, I most certainly would have.

To all of Josh's classmates and the Grey Nun Academy community. Your daily calls, notes, gifts and prayers were a welcomed distraction for Josh when he was ill. You made him look forward to each day; it was something he cherished.

To Erin and Austin, this book is dedicated to the two of you. It is hard growing up without the brother who you both looked up to. But the two of you possess the same compassion for people and life that Josh did. We are so proud to be your parents.

To all of Josh's friends, cousins, team mates, classmates, teachers, coaches, neighbors and relatives. Everyone was so supportive through his life and brief ordeal, and he always wanted to thank everyone in a big way. I guess the book and the way he now communicates is his thank you to everyone.

To the Philly Friends of V for honoring Josh annually along with so many other great friends and acquaintances who cancer has affected in our community. Being on the basketball court is what he was all about. There is no better way to honor him than through these four special days.

And to Marie…you have a remarkable talent. You were able to take words and transform them into a beautiful true story of Josh's life and how he continues to send us feathers and messages of love. You are his messenger. I guess that is why you were one of the first he came to in a dream. He knew you would tell his story. We are forever grateful. Thank you.

Author's Note

You will notice that it took a very long time from the day this book was started until it went into print. It took me a while to write it for various reasons, then there were new messages from Joshua to add, and editing to be made (I'd like to thank Kathleen Pisauro for her excellent copyediting - she's brilliant). But what has taken the longest is trying to get permission to use the lyrics to Lacy's Song which was originally included in the manuscript in its entirety. Unfortunately, I was unable to secure that permission.

I put the book in a PDF on my website, and when the Wilkers knew of people who needed comfort, they led them to the site. Through word-of-mouth the demand for the book—a real book in print or in Kindle format—has grown. People have been asking the Wilkers where they can purchase numerous copies to give out.

And to be honest, Joshua has been "whispering in my ear" to get the book done once and for all. So we've left the lyrics to Buddy Jewell's song out. Please take a moment to look them up or listen to them, and you'll see why they were so important to that part of the story.

It is with relief and great joy that Joshua's Ring is being released. Also, and in truth, I didn't realize this until after the book was complete, the total page count is 56 from the very first to the very last page—5 + 6 = 11—he never stops, does he? I have found feathers in the least expected places—on my breakfast plate on Christmas morning after a sleepless night thinking that I HAD to get Joshua's Ring published soon, and one floated from a cabinet that holds nothing but dishes on the very day I completed this version of the book. I have a feeling I won't be receiving his feathers now that the book is published. I'll miss them. His story is told now. It's bittersweet for me, as I'm sure it is for his parents.

It was an honor and a privelege to be asked to write this book for Rosemary and Joe. It has given me some of the most profoundly spiritual moments in my life. It is humbling to have their trust and confidence. I'm not certain I deserve it. I thank them for being such tremendous role models...and for being such darn good people.

Marie Duess, January 2013

For more information about **Joshua's Ring**, or to get permission to use it in part or whole, please visit www.MarieDuess.com/Joshua_s_Ring.html or www.JoshuasRing.com

Made in the USA
Lexington, KY
02 June 2013